To _____

_____

From _____

Date _____

Baby Names Book

illustrated by FRANK ENDERSBY

Ladybird Books

Boys

Aaron: (Hebrew) 'lofty', 'mountaineer'.

Abdul: (Arabic) 'servant of'.

Abraham: (Hebrew) 'father of many'. Pet forms: Abe, Abie, Bram, Ham.

Adam: (Hebrew) 'red earth'.

Adrian: (Latin) 'man from Adria'. Other form: Hadrian (Roman).

Alan: Origin disputed. Possibly (Irish) 'noble' or (Welsh) 'harmony'. Other forms: Allan, Allen, Alun.

Alastair: (Gaelic) from the Greek name **Alexander**, meaning 'defender of men'. Other forms: Alasdair, Alistair, Alister, Allie, Ally.

Albert: (Old German) 'noble' and 'bright'. Other forms: Al, Alberto (Italian and Spanish), Aubert, Bert, Bertie, Halbert.

Alec, Alex: See **Alexander**.

Alexander: (Greek) 'defender of men'. One of the oldest recorded names, kept popular through saints and kings. Other forms: Alastair (Scottish), Alec, Alex, Alexis (Russian), Alic(k), Eck, Ecky, Sacha, Sanders, Sandy, Sasha.

Alfred: (Old German) 'elf counsel' or 'good counsellor'. Other forms: Alf, Alfie, Fred.

Amos: (Hebrew) 'strong, bearing a burden'.

Andrew: (Greek) 'manly'. One of the most popular names in Britain, especially in Scotland because of the patron saint of that name. Other forms: Anderson, Andreas. Pet forms: Andie, Andy, Drew.

Angus: (Celtic) from the Gaelic name *Aonghus*, meaning 'one choice'. Popular in Scotland.

Anthony: (Latin) from *Antonius*, the name of a Roman clan. Other forms: Anton (German), Antony, Tony.

Arnold: (Old German) 'eagle' or 'strength'.

Arthur: Origin disputed. Possibly (Irish) 'stone' or (Celtic) 'bear'. Made famous through the legend of King Arthur and his Knights. Other forms: Art, Artie.

Ashley: (Old English) 'ash wood'.

B

Barnabas: (Hebrew) 'son of exhortation' – implying that the child is an answer to prayers. Other forms: Barnaby, Barney, Barnie.

Barry, Barrie: (Irish) 'spear'. Also the pet form of **Finbar** and **Henry**.

Bartholomew: (Hebrew) 'son of Talmai'. Other forms: Bart, Bartie, Bartlet, Bartlemy, Bartley.

Basil: (Greek) 'kingly'.

Ben: (Hebrew) 'son' or (Gaelic) 'peak, mountain'. Also pet form of **Benedict** and **Benjamin**.

Benedict: (Latin) 'blessed'. Other forms: **Ben**, Benett, Bennet, Benny.

Benjamin: (Hebrew) 'son of the right hand' – implying son of good fortune. Pet forms: **Ben**, Benjie, Bennie.

Bernard: (Old German) 'bear-hard' – implying strength and courage. Other forms: Barnardin, Barnard, Barny, Bernhard, Bjorn (Swedish).

Bertram: (Old German) 'bright raven'. Pet forms: Bert, Bertie.

Boris: (Russian) 'fight'.

Bradley: (Old English) 'broad clearing'. Other forms: Brad, Braden, Brady, Broderick.

Brendan: (Irish) meaning is uncertain. Possibly 'dweller by the beacon' or 'stinking hair'. Other forms: Brandon, Brendon, Dan.

Brett: (Latin) from the surname, meaning 'a Breton'.

Brian: (Celtic) of uncertain meaning. Possibly 'hill' or 'strength'. Other forms: Briant, Briar, Brien, Bryan, Bryon.

Bruce: (Old French) 'brushwood thicket'.

Bruno: (Old German) 'brown, bear-like'.

Bryn: (Welsh) 'hill'.

C

Calum, Callum: (Gaelic) from the Latin name *Columba*, meaning 'dove'. Also used as a pet form of **Malcolm**.

Calvin: Origin disputed. Possibly (Latin) 'bald' or from the surname of the 16th century French religious reformer *John Calvin*.

Cameron: (Gaelic) 'crooked nose'.

Campbell: (Celtic) 'curved mouth'.

Carl, Karl: See **Charles**.

Cary: See **Charles**.

Caspar: See **Jasper**.

Cecil: (Latin) 'blind'.

Cedric: The name of a character in Sir Walter Scott's novel *Ivanhoe* (1819). It is said that Scott mistook the name for *Cerdic*, the name of the first King of Wessex.

Charles: (Old German) 'man'. Other forms: Carel, Carl, Karl (German), Carlie, Carlton, Carlyle, Carol (French), Cary, Chad, Charlie, Chas, Chick, Chuck, Karel, Siari (Welsh).

Christian: (Latin) 'follower of Christ'. The name of the hero of John Bunyan's *Pilgrim's Progress*. Other forms: Chris, Christy, Kris, Kristian (German).

Christopher: (Greek) 'bearer of Christ'. *St Christopher*, who is the patron saint of travellers, is said to have carried the infant Christ across a river to safety.
Other forms: Christoph, Kris, Kristofer (German), Christophe (French).
Pet forms: Chip, Chris, Christy, Kit.

Clarence: The dukes of Clarence were named after the Suffolk town *Clare,* which was named after the Norman family *de Clare.*
Other forms: Claron, Sinclair.

Clark: (Old English) 'learned man'. Originally the name for the church scholars, who were the only people who could read and write.

Claud(e): (Latin) 'lame'. From the Roman emperor *Claudius,* who walked with a limp.

Clement: (Latin) 'mild' or 'merciful'.

Clifford: (German) 'dweller on a slope'.
Pet form: Cliff.

Clint, Clinton: Derived from a place-name, meaning 'settlement near a hill'.

Clive: Derived from a place-name, meaning 'cliff'. Originally a surname, but gained popularity as a first name after *Sir Robert Clive,* the British soldier and statesman who was known as 'Clive of India'.

Colin, Colan: (Gaelic) 'a young dog' or 'youth'. Also a shortened form of **Nicholas.**

Conan: (Celtic) 'high' or 'wisdom'.

Conrad: (German) 'bold in counsel'.
Other forms: Conrade, Curt, Konrad, Kurt.

Craig: (Gaelic) 'rock'.

Crispin: (Latin) 'curly-haired'.
Other forms: Crispian, Crispinian.

Curt: See **Conrad.**

Curtis: (Old French) 'courteous'.

Cyril: (Greek) 'lord, master'.

D

Damian: (Greek) 'tamer'.
Other forms: Damien, Damion.

Daniel: (Hebrew) 'God has judged'.
Pet forms: Dan, Danny.

Darrel: (Old English) 'darling'.
Other forms: Darrell, Darrol, Daryl.

Darren: (Irish) 'dearly beloved'.
Other forms: Darran, Darien, Darrin, Darryn.

David: (Hebrew) 'beloved'. The name of the patron saint of Wales, and one of the top ten boys' names since the 1950s. Other forms: Dafydd, Dai, Dave, Davie, Davy, Taffy.

Dean: Origin disputed. Possibly (Old English) 'valley' or (Latin) 'leader of ten'.

Denis: (Greek) derived from *Dionysus*, the Greek god of wine and revelry.
Other forms: Den, Dennis, Denny.

Derek: (Old German) derived from the name *Theodoric*, meaning 'people rule'. Other forms: Deric, Derrick, Derry, Deryk, Dirk, Rick.

Dermot: (Irish) 'free from envy'. Other forms: Dermott, Diamaid, Diamid, Diamit.

Desmond: (Irish) derived from the Irish surname, meaning 'a man from South Munster'. Pet forms: Des, Desie.

Dominic, Dominick: (Latin) 'born on the Sabbath day'. Pet form: Dom.

Donald: (Celtic) from the Gaelic name *Domhnall*, meaning 'world mighty'.
Other forms: Don, Donal (Irish), Donnie, Donny.

Douglas: (Celtic) 'dark water'. A Scottish clan name, and once the name of a Celtic river. Pet forms: Doug, Dougie, Douggie.

Dudley: Originally a surname derived from the place-name in Worcestershire.

Duncan: (Celtic) from the Gaelic name *Donnchadh*, meaning 'brown warrior'.

Dwight: Derived from an English surname.

Dylan: (Welsh) 'son of the sea'.

Eamon: See **Edmund**.

Earl: (Old English) 'noble' or 'chief'.
Other form: Errol (German).

Edgar: (Old English) 'happy spear'.
Other form: Eadgar.

Edmund: (Old English) 'happy protection'.
Other forms: Eamon (Irish), Edmond (French).

Edward: (Old English) 'rich guardian'.
A common royal choice of name since Saxon times. Pet forms: Ed, Eddie, Eddy, Ned, Neddie, Neddy, Ted, Teddie, Teddy.

Edwin: (Old English) 'rich friend'. The Scottish capital city, Edinburgh, is said to derive from *Edwin's burgh* (Edwin's town).

Eli, Ely: (Hebrew) 'height'. Other forms: Eliot, Eliott, Elliot, Elliott (Scottish).

Eliot: See **Eli**.

Emlyn: (Welsh) of uncertain meaning. Possibly derived from the Latin name *Aemilius*, or (Old German) 'serpent of work'.

Enoch: (Hebrew) 'dedicated'.

Eric: (Old Norse) 'sole ruler'.

Ernest: (Old German) 'vigour' or 'earnestness'. Other forms: Ern, Ernie, Ernst (German).

Errol: See **Earl**.

Esau: (Hebrew) 'hairy'.

Eugene: (Greek) 'well-born'. Other form: Gene.

Eustace: (Greek) 'rich in corn'. Other form: Stacey.

Evan: See **John** and **Ewen**.

Ewen: (Celtic) derived from the Irish name *Eoghan*, meaning 'a youth'. Other forms: Evan, Ewan, Owen (Welsh).

Fabian: (Latin) 'bean-grower'.

Felix: (Latin) 'happy'.

Fergus: (Gaelic) 'man's choice'.

Finbar: (Gaelic) 'fair head'. Pet form: Barry.

Finlay: (Gaelic) 'a sunbeam'. Other forms: Findlay, Findley.

Finn: (Gaelic) 'fair'.

Fitzroy: (Latin) 'illegitimate son of a king'.

Francis: (Latin) 'Frenchman'. Other forms: Francesco (Italian), Francisco (Spanish), François (French), Franz (German). Pet forms: Frank, Francie, Frankie.

Fraser: A surname adopted as a first name. May have begun as a French place-name or possibly derived from the French word *fraise*, meaning 'strawberry'.

Frederick: (Old German) 'peaceful ruler'. Other forms: Frédéric (French), Fritz (German). Pet forms: Fred, Freddie, Freddy.

Gareth: (Welsh) 'gentle'. Other forms: **Gary**, Garry, Garth.

Garfield: (Old English) 'spear field'. Pet form: **Gary**.

Garret: See **Gerard**.

Garth: See **Gareth** and **Garard**.

Gary: A short form of **Gareth**, **Gerald** and **Garfield** or possibly from the German name *Garvey*, meaning 'spear-bearer'.

Gavin: (Welsh) 'hawk of May'.

Gene: See **Eugene**.

Geoffrey, Jeffrey: (Old German) 'district peace'. Popular in the Middle Ages, and led to many surnames, like *Jeffries* and *Jeeves*. Pet forms: Geoff, Jeff.

George: (Greek) 'farmer'. The name of the patron saint of England. Other forms: Georg (German), Georges (French), Giorgio (Italian), Jorge (Spanish). Pet form: Georgie.

Gerald: (Old German) 'spear ruler'. Other forms: **Gary**, Gerrie, Gerry, Gerold, Jerald, Jerold.

Gerard: (Old German) 'spear hard'. Other forms: Garret (Irish), Garth.

Gilbert: (Old German) 'bright pledge'. Pet forms: Bert, Bertie, Gib, Gibby, Gil.

Giles: Origin disputed. Possibly (Latin) 'kid-like' or (Celtic) 'servant'.

Glen, Glenn: (Welsh) began as a surname, meaning 'from the valley'.

Glyn: (Celtic) 'small valley'.

Godfrey: (Old German) 'God's peace'.

Gordon: Originally a Scottish surname, but popular as a first name since the 1880s.

Graham: Originally an English place-name. It was adopted in Scotland as a clan name, but has been used as a first name since medieval times. Other forms: Graeme, Grahame.

Grant: Derived from the surname, which developed from the French *le grand* (the big). Often a nickname applied to a tall man.

Gregory: (Greek) 'watchman'. Other forms: Greg, Gregg, Gregor, Grig.

Griffith: (Welsh) 'reddish'. Derived from the Welsh name *Gruffydd* ('-ydd' meaning 'land').

Guy: (Old German) 'wood' or 'wide'. Original form *Wido*, adopted by the Italians as *Guido*, then by the French as **Guy**.

Hamish: The anglicised form of **Seamas** and **Seumas**, which are Gaelic forms of **James**.

Hank: See **Henry**.

Hans: See **John**.

Harold, Harald: (Old Norse) 'army power'. Pet form: Harry.

Harrison: See **Henry**.

Harvey: (French) 'battleworthy'. Pet forms: Harve, Herve.

Hayden: Originally a place-name meaning 'pasture land', then a surname, now used as a first name for both boys and girls. Other forms: Haydn, Haydon.

Hector: (Greek) 'hold fast'. Other forms: Heck, Hektor.

Henry: (Old German) 'home ruler'. The name has been popular since the Middle Ages. **Harry** was the original English form, from the French *Henri*. Other forms: Barry, Hadrick, Hal, Hank, Harrison, Harry, Hendrick, Henri, Heriot.

Herbert: (Old German) 'bright army'. Pet forms: Bert, Bertie, Herbie.

Hew: See **Hugh**.

Hilary: (Latin) 'cheerful'.

Hiram, Hyram: (Hebrew) 'noble'.

Horace, Horatio: (Latin) 'punctual'.

Howard: A surname used as a first name. Of uncertain meaning. Possibly 'a guardian of an enclosure' or (Old German) 'heart protection'.

Hugh: (Old German) 'bright mind'.
Other forms: Hew, Huw (Welsh), Hubert,
Hughie, Hugo.

Humphrey, Humfrey: (Old English) 'giant
peace'. Pet forms: Hum, Hump, Humpie,
Humps, Numps.

Iain, Ian: See **John**.

Ik, Ike, Iky: See **Isaac**.

Innes, Innis: (Gaelic) 'island'. Scottish
place-name and surname, used in Scotland as
a first name for boys and girls.

Innocent: (Latin) 'harmless, innocent'.

Ira: (Hebrew) 'watchful'.

Irving, Irvin: Derived from the Scottish place-
name and surname, meaning 'fair, handsome'.

Isaac, Izaak: (Hebrew) 'laughter'.
Pet forms: Ik, Ike, Iky.

Ivan: See **John**.

Ivor: Precise origin uncertain. Possibly from
the Old Norse name *Ivarr* and connected with
the Norse hero, *Ing*. Or from the Welsh name
Ifor, meaning 'lord'.
Or possibly from a
Germanic root
meaning 'yew'.
Other forms: Ives,
Ivon, Yves
(French).

Jack: Pet form of **John** and **Jacob**, used as a
name in its own right. In the Middle Ages the
name was so common that it was used
generally to mean 'a man', hence *Jack Tar*,
Jack Frost, *Jack of all trades*.
Pet form: Jacky.

Jacob: (Hebrew) 'supplanter' or 'deceiver'.
Other forms: Jack, Jacques (French), Jake.

Jake: See **Jacob**.

James: (Hebrew) 'supplanter'. A corruption of
the name **Jacob**. It has been the most popular
British boys' name for over twenty years.
Other forms: Diego, Jaime (Spanish), Seamas,
Seumas (Gaelic), Hamish, Jeames (Scottish).
Pet forms: Jamie, Jamy, Jim, Jimmy.

Jan: See **John**.

Jared, Jarod: (Hebrew) 'descent'.

Jason: (Greek) 'a healer'. Or possibly the
Greek form of the Hebrew name **Joshua**.

Jasper: (Persian) 'treasure holder'.
Other forms: Caspar (German), Gasper,
Jaspar, Kaspar.

Jay: From the bird which may derive from the
Latin name *Gaius*, meaning 'to rejoice'.

Jed: (Hebrew) 'friend of the Lord'. Pet form of
the name *Jedidiah*, now more commonly used
as a name in its own right.

Jeff, Jeffrey: See **Geoffrey**.

Jeremy: (Old English) from the Hebrew name *Jeremiah*, meaning 'God is on high'.
Pet form: Jerry.

Jerome, Jerram: From the Greek name *Hieronymus*, meaning 'holy name'.

Jesse: (Hebrew) 'God exists'.

Jethro: (Hebrew) 'abundance' and 'excellence'.
Pet forms: Jeth, Jett.

Jock: See **John.** Sometimes a name given to a Scotsman.

Joe: See **Joseph.**

Joel: (Hebrew) 'Jehovah is God'.

John: (Hebrew) 'God is gracious'. **John** is found in various forms throughout Europe, and has been one of the most popular boys' names since the 17th century. Other forms: Giovanni (Italian), Jan (Dutch), Iain, Ian (Scottish), Evan, Ieuan, Sion (Welsh), Ivan, Vanya (Russian), Jean (French), Johann(es) (German), Juan (Spanish), Sean (Irish), Shane, Shann, Shawn. Pet forms: Hans (German), Jack, Jackie, Jan, Jock (Scottish), Jonnie, Johnny.

Jonah: (Hebrew) 'dove'.
Other form: Jonas (Greek).

Jonathan: (Hebrew) 'God has given'.
Pet forms: Jon, Jonny.

Jordan: (Hebrew) 'flowing down'. The name of the main river in the Holy Land.

Joseph: (Hebrew) 'God shall add'.
Pet forms: Jo, Joe, Joey, Jos.

Joshua: (Hebrew) 'God is my saviour'.
Pet form: Josh.

Julian: (Latin) 'belonging to *Julius*'.
Other forms: Jolin, Jolyon, Jules.

Justin: (Latin) 'righteous, just'.

Kane: Origin uncertain. Possibly derived from the Celtic name *MacCathain* (cath meaning warrior) or from the French place-name *Caen*, which means 'field of combat'.

Kaspar: See **Jasper.**

Keith: A Scottish surname derived from a place-name, probably from the Gaelic word for 'wood' or 'windy place', now used as a first name.

Kelvin: Origin uncertain. Possibly from the name of the Scottish river, or from two Old English words meaning 'ship' and 'friend'.

Ken: See **Kenneth.**

Kenneth: (Gaelic) 'handsome'.
Other forms: Cenydd (Welsh), Kevan, Kevin (Irish). Pet forms: Ken, Kenny.

Kevin, Kevan: See **Kenneth.**

Kieran, Kieren: (Irish) 'little dark one'.

Kim: (Old English) 'royally bold'.
Also a girl's name.

Kingsley: (Old English) 'king's wood' or 'king's meadow'. A surname now used as a first name.

Kirk: (Old Norse) 'church'.

Kit: See **Christopher.**

Kris: See **Christian** and **Christopher**.

Kurt: See **Conrad**.

Lance: (Old German) 'land'. A shortened and more commonly used form of *Lancelot*.

Larry: See **Laurence**.

Laurence, Lawrence: (Latin) 'of Laurentium' – a town which took its name from the laurel plant, symbolising victory. Pet forms: Lanty, Larkin, Larry, Laurie.

Lawson: English surname used as a first name since the 1850s, meaning 'son of Lawrence'.

Lee, Leigh: (Old English) 'meadow'. A surname now used as a first name.

Leo: (Latin) 'lion'. The fifth sign of the zodiac. Other forms: Leon, Lionel, Llew (Welsh).

Leon: See **Leo**.

Leonard, Lennard: (Old German) 'strong as a lion'. Pet forms: Len, Lenn, Lennie, Lenny, Lorrie.

Leroy: (Old French) 'the king'. Originally used as a surname for someone connected with the king's household.

Leslie: Scottish place-name and surname now used as a first name. **Lesley** is the feminine form. Pet form: Les.

Lester: The phonetic form of the English place-name *Leicester*. A surname used as a first name since the 19th century.

Lewis: (Celtic) 'lionlike'. Anglicised from the French **Louis**. Pet forms: Lew, Lewie, Louie.

Liam: See **William**.

Lindsay: Scottish place-name and surname, now used as a first name. **Lindsey** is the female equivalent. Other forms: Lyndsay, Lynsay.

Linus: (Greek) 'flax'.

Lionel: (Latin) 'little lion'.

Llew: See **Leo**.

Lloyd: (Welsh) 'grey'.

Louis: (French) 'famous'. Pet forms: Lou, Louie.

Lucas: (Latin) 'man from Lucania' – a place in Southern Italy. Originally a surname, but in use as a first name since the 1930s. Other form: Luke.

Luke: See **Lucas**.

Luther: (Old German) 'famous warrior'. Its use as a first name dates from the German religious reformer *Martin Luther* (1483-1546).

Magnus: (Latin) 'great'.

Malcolm: From the Gaelic *Maol Caluim*, meaning 'servant of Columba'.

Manuel, Manoel: (Hebrew) 'God with us'. Pet form: Manny.

Marcus: (Latin) derived from *Mars*, the Roman god of war. Other forms: Marc, Marcel (French), March, Marion, Marius (Italian), Mark (English).

Mark: See **Marcus**.

Marlon: See **Mervin**.

Martin, Martyn: (Latin) deriving from the name *Martinus*, which means 'belonging to Mars'. Pet forms: Martie, Marty.

Matthew, Mathew: (Hebrew) 'gift of the Lord'. Pet forms: Mat, Matt.

Maurice, Morris: (Latin) 'dark-skinned'. Other forms: Menrig (Welsh), Merrick, Meyrick (English).

Max: Pet form of names beginning with 'Max –', also used independently since the 1880s.

Maximilian: (Latin) 'greatest'. Other forms: Maxime (French), Maxwell (English). Pet forms: **Max**, Maxie.

Maxwell: See **Maximilian**.

Melvin, Melvyn: Origins uncertain. Possibly (Celtic) 'chief' or (Gaelic) 'smooth brow'. Pet form: Mel.

Mervin, Mervyn: From the Welsh name *Myrddin*, meaning 'sea-hill'. Other forms: Marlon, Marvyn, Merle, Merlin, Merlon.

Micah: (Hebrew) shortened form of *Micaiah* now used as a name in its own right.

Michael: (Greek) from the Hebrew *Micaiah*, meaning 'Who is like the Lord?' One of the most popular boys' names. Pet forms: Mick, Mike, Mickie, Micky.

Miles, Myles: Uncertain origin. Possibly (Old German) 'generous' or (Greek) 'millstone'.

Moray, Murray: (Celtic) 'sea'. A place-name and surname, now used as a first name.

Morgan: (Welsh) 'sea dweller'.

Morris: See **Maurice**.

Moses: Possibly (Hebrew) 'delivered' (from water) or (Egyptian) 'child, son'.

Mungo: (Gaelic) 'amiable'. The nickname of *St Kentigern*, the patron saint of Glasgow.

Murray: See **Moray**.

N

Nahum: (Hebrew) 'consoling'.

Nathan: (Hebrew) 'gift'. Pet forms: Nat, Natty.

Nathanael, Nathaniel: (Hebrew) 'gift of God'. Pet forms: Nat, Natty.

Neal, Neil, Niall: See **Nigel**.

Nelson: Originally a surname meaning 'Neil's son'. Became popular as a first name after *Lord Nelson*, the great British sailor.

Neville, Nevil: From a French place-name meaning 'new town'. Originally a surname brought to Britain by the Normans, used as a first name since the 1860s.

Nicholas: (Greek) 'victory of the people'. The name of the patron saint of children, often known as Father Christmas or Santa Claus. Pet forms: Colin, Colan, Nick, Nicky.

Nigel: Possibly (Irish) 'champion' or (Latin) 'black'. Other forms: Neal, Neil, Niall.

Noah: (Hebrew) 'rest'.

Noel: (French) 'Christ's birthday', 'Christmas'. Originally both a male and female name, but used more for boys since the 17th century.

Nolan, Nolen: (Irish) 'shout' or 'famous'.

Norman: (Old English) 'man from the North' or 'Norwegian'. Pet form: Norm.

Norris: Possibly (French) 'nurse' or (Old English) 'Northerner'.

Olav: (Old Norse) 'ancestor'. A favourite Scandinavian name, also popular in Scotland and Ireland. Other forms: Ola, Ole, Olaf.

Oliver: Origin uncertain. Possibly (French) 'olive tree' or (Old German) 'elf host'.

Omar: (Arabic) 'eloquent'.

Oran: (Irish) 'green'.

Orson: (Latin) 'bear'.

Oscar: (Old English) 'divine spear'.

Oswald: (Old English) 'divine power'.

Otis: See **Otto**.

Otto: (Old German) 'possessions' or 'rich'. Other forms: Odo, Otho, Otis.

Owen: (Welsh) 'well-born'. Other forms: Ewan, Ewen, Oswain.

Parry: See **Peter**.

Pascal: (French) 'Easter'. Used for children born around the time of Easter.

Patrick: (Latin) 'noble man'. The name of the patron saint of Ireland, where it is still one of the most common names. Other forms: Padraig (Irish), Patrice (French). Pet forms: Paddy, Pat.

Paul: (Latin) 'small'. One of the top ten boys' names in Britain.

Perceval, Percival: (French) 'penetrate the valley'. Pet forms: Perce, Percy.

Percy: Pet form of **Percival**, but also long established as a name in its own right. Derived from a Norman place-name, it was used originally as a surname in England.

Peter: (Greek) 'stone, rock'. Other forms: Parnell, Parry, Pete, Pier, Piers, Pierre (French), Rockie.

Phelan: (Irish) 'wolf'.

Phil(l)ip: (Greek) 'fond of horses'. One of the most popular boys' names. Pet form: Phil.

Phineas: (Hebrew) 'oracle'.

Pierce, Pierre, Piers: See **Peter**.

Preston: English place-name and surname, meaning 'priest's statement' or 'priest's song'. Used as a first name since the 1860s.

Quentin, Quintin: (Latin) 'fifth'. A name often given to the fifth-born child.

Quincy: French place-name, meaning 'estate belonging to Quintus'.

Quinn: (Irish) 'counsel'.

Ralf, Ralph: (Old English) 'wolf-counsel'. *Radulf* was the original form.
Other forms: Rafe, Raoul (French).

Ramsay, Ramsey: English place-name and Scottish surname, used as a first name since the 19th century.

Randolph, Randolf: (Old English) 'shield-wolf'. Other forms: Ran, Rand, Randel, Rando, Randy.

Raoul: See **Ralf**.

Ray: See **Raymond**.

Raymond: (Old German) 'counsel' or 'protector'. Other forms: Ray, Redmond (Irish).

Rayner, Rainer: (Old German) 'mighty army'.

Redmond: See **Raymond**.

Reese: See **Rhys**.

Regan: (Irish) derived from the Irish surname *O'Riaggin*, meaning 'descendant of the little king'.

Reginald, Reynold, Ronald, Ranald: (Old German) 'power force'. Pet forms: Reg, Reggie, Rex, Ron, Ronnie.

Reuben: (Hebrew) 'behold a son'.

Rex: (Latin) 'king'. Also a pet form of **Reginald**.

Reynold: See **Reginald**.

Rhys, Reese: (Welsh) 'ardour' or 'rashness'.

Richard: (Old German) 'strong ruler'. Pet forms: Dick, Dickie, Dicken, Dickon, Dicky, Hick, Rick, Richie.

Robert: (Old German) 'fame, bright'. Pet forms: Bert, Bertie, Bob, Bobbie, Bobby, Dob, Dobbin, Rab, Rabbie (Scottish), Rob, Robbie, Robin, Rupert (German).

Robin, Robyn: See **Robert**.

Roderick: (Old German) 'famous rule'. Also the anglicised form of the Gaelic name *Ruaridh*, meaning 'red'. Pet forms: Rod, Roddy.

Rodney: (Old English) 'reed island'. Pet forms: Rod, Rodders, Roddy.

Roger: (Old German) 'famous spear'.

Roland, Rowland: (Old German) 'famous land'.

Rolf(e), Rolph: See **Rudolf**.

Ron, Ronald: See **Reginald**.

Rory, Rorier: (Gaelic) 'red'.

Ross: (Gaelic) 'peninsula'.

Rowan: (Irish) 'little red one'.

Rowland: See **Roland**.

Roy: (Gaelic) 'red'.

Rudolf, Rudolph: (Old German) 'famed wolf'. Pet forms: Rolf(e), Rollo, Rolph, Rudi, Rudy.

Rufus: (Latin) 'red-haired'.

Rupert: See **Robert**.

Russel, Russell: From the French nickname indicating 'a man with red hair' or 'red-faced'. Pet form: Russ.

Ryan: (Irish) 'little king'.

Sam: See **Samson** and **Samuel**.

Samson, Sampson: (Hebrew) 'child of the sun'. Pet form: Sam.

Samuel: (Hebrew) 'heard by God'. Pet form: Sam.

Sandy: See **Alexander**.

Saul: (Hebrew) 'asked for'.

Scott: A surname meaning 'man from Scotland', used since the 1940s as a first name.

Seamas, Seumas: See **James**.

Sean: See **John**.

Sebastian: (Latin) 'man from Sebastia' – a place in Turkey. Pet forms: Bastian, Seb.

Seth: (Hebrew) 'appointed'.

Seymour: Originally a Norman place-name and noble surname, meaning 'the sower'.

Shane, Shann, Shawn: English form of the Irish name **Sean**. See **John**.

Shelly: English place-name and surname, meaning 'meadow on a slope or ledge'. Used as a first name for boys and girls.

Sherlock: (Old English) 'fair-haired'.

Sholto: (Greek) 'sower'.

Siari: See **Charles**.

Sidney, Sydney: Possibly from the French place-name *Saint Denis*, brought to Britain by the Normans, or from a place in Surrey, called *La Sydenye*, meaning 'wide, well-watered land'. Pet forms: Sid, Syd.

Sigmund: (German) 'victory shield'.

Silas, Sylas: From the Greek name *Silonanos*, deriving from the Latin name *Silvannus*, meaning 'dweller in the woods'. Other forms: Silvanus, Silvester, Sylvester, Silvius, Sylvius.

Silvester, Sylvester: See **Silas**.

Simeon: (Hebrew) 'listening attentively'.

Simon: (Greek) 'snub-nosed'. Pet forms: Si, Sim, Simmy, Simkin.

Sion: See **John**.

Solomon: (Hebrew) 'peace'. Pet forms: Sol, Solly.

Sonny, Sonnie, Sunny: Originally a name given to mean 'boy', now used as a name in its own right.

Spencer: Originally a surname deriving from the job of 'dispensing provisions', for example, a butler. Used as a first name since the 1930s.

Stacey: See **Eustace**.

Stanley: From the surname and English place-name, meaning 'stony clearing'. Pet form: Stan.

Stephen, Steven: (Greek) 'crown'. One of the most popular boys' names. Other forms: Stefan, Stephan (German), Steven. Pet forms: Steenie, Steve, Stevie.

Stewart, Stuart: (Old English) 'household servant'.

Sydney: See **Sidney**.

Sylvester: See **Silas**.

Terence: (Latin) 'tender', from the Roman clan name. Pet form: Terry.

Terry: See **Terence**.

Tex: From the name of the American state *Texas*.

Theo: Used as a first name in its own right and also a pet form of names beginning with 'Theo –'.

Theodore: (Greek) 'God's gift'. Pet forms: Theo, Tudor (Welsh).

Thomas: (Hebrew) 'twin'. A popular boys' name since the 12th century. Other forms: Tam, Tammie (Scottish), Thompson, Tom, Tomas, Tommy.

Thurstan: (Old German) 'Thor's stone'. In German mythology, *Thor* was a great warrior, represented as a red-bearded man of enormous strength.

Tim: See **Timothy**.

Timothy: (Greek) 'honouring God'. A popular name since the 1930s. Pet forms: Tim, Timmy.

Tobias: (Hebrew) 'God is good'. Pet form: Toby.

Toby: See **Tobias**.

Tommy: See **Thomas**. Also the nickname given to British soldiers, dating back to the 19th century, when the specimen signature on the enlistment form was *Tommy Atkin*.

Tony: See **Anthony**.

Torquil: (Old Norse) derived from the name of the legendary god, *Thor*.

Travis, Travers: From the surname, meaning 'toll collector'.

Trevor: (Irish) 'prudent, wise'. Other form: Trefor (Welsh).

Tristan, Tristram, Tristrem: (Celtic) 'tumult'.

Tudor: See **Theodore**.

Ullrick, Ulrich: (Old English) 'wolf-powerful'.

Uriah: (Hebrew) 'my light is the Lord'.

Val: See **Valentine**.

Valentine: (Latin) 'to be strong'. A 3rd century saint whose martyrdom on 14th February coincided with a pagan love festival – hence St Valentine's Day.

Vance: From the English surname, meaning 'someone who has lived near a marsh or fen'.

Vanya: See **John**.

Vaughan: (Welsh) from the surname, meaning 'little'. Used as a first name since the late 19th century.

Verdon, Verdun: From the French place-name.

Vernon: French place-name and English surname, meaning 'alder tree'. Used as a first name from the early 19th century.

Victor: (Latin) 'conqueror'.

Vince, Vincent: (Latin) 'to conquer'.

Virgil: (Latin) from the Roman clan name *Vergilius*.

Vivian: (Latin) 'living, alive' or possibly from the Roman clan name *Vibius*.

Wallace, Wallis: (Celtic) 'Welshman'. Pet form: Wally.

Walter: (Old German) 'ruling people'. Pet forms: Wally, Walt.

Ward: From the surname, meaning 'guardian'.

Warren: Introduced by the Normans as a surname, now used as a first name.

Wayne: From the surname, meaning 'wagon maker'.

Wesley: From the surname and English place-name, meaning 'west meadow'.

Wilbert: (Old English) 'well-bright'.

Wilbur, Wilber: A surname used as a first name.

Wilfred, Wilfrid: (Old English) 'resolute, peaceful'. Pet forms: Wilf, Will.

Will: See **William**.

William: (Old German) 'resolute protector'. Introduced to Britain by the Normans in the 11th century and still one of the most popular boys' names. Other forms: Bill, Billy, Liam (Irish), Will, Willie, Willis, Willy, Wilmot, Wilson.

Wilmer, Willmer: (Old German) from *Willimar*, meaning 'resolute, famous'.

Wilmot: See **William**.

Winfred: (Old English) 'friend, peace'.

Winston: A place-name and surname, now used as a first name.

Xavier: (Arabic) 'splendid'. Other form: Zavier.

Yehudi: (Hebrew) 'praise of the Lord'.

Yul: (Mongolian) 'beyond the horizon'.

Zachariah: (Hebrew) 'God has remembered'. Other forms: Zach, Zacchaeus, Zaccheus, Zacharias, Zachary, Zak, Zechariah.

Zedekiah: (Hebrew) 'God is righteousness'.

Girls

Abigail: (Hebrew) 'father rejoices'.
Pet forms: Abbey, Abbie, Gail.

Adelaide: Anglicised form of the Old German *Adelheid*, meaning 'noble, kind'. Pet forms: Ada, Ade, Heidi (German).

Adeline, Adelina: (Old German) 'noble'.
Pet forms: Addy, Aline.

Adriana, Adrienne: (Latin) 'woman from Adria'. The feminine version of **Adrian**.

Agnes: (Greek) 'pure'. Other forms: Agnese (Italian), Agneta, Annes, Annice, Annis, Ines, Inez (Spanish). Pet forms: Aggie, Nance, Nancy, Nessa, Nessie, Nesta.

Aileen: See **Helen**.

Ailsa: From the *Ailsa Craig* island rock in the Firth of Clyde, Scotland.

Aimee: See **Amy**.

Alethea: (Greek) 'truth'. Other forms: Alethia, Aletia.

Alexandra: (Greek) 'defender of men'. The feminine version of **Alexander**. Other forms: Alexa, Alix, Sacha, Sandra, Sandy, Zandra.

Alexis: (Greek) 'helper' or 'defender'.

Alice: (Old German) 'truth' and 'nobility'. The old form was *Adelice* or *Adelise*. Other forms: Ailie, Alicia, Alisa, Alison. Pet forms: Allie, Aly.

Aline: See **Adeline**.

Alison: Originally the Scottish form of **Alice**, now a name in its own right.

Amanda: From the Latin, meaning 'lovable', although probably a literary invention.
Pet forms: Manda, Mandy.

Amelia: Possibly from an Old German word meaning 'labour', or from the Latin *aemilius*, meaning 'industrious'. Pet forms: Millie, Milly.

Amy: (French) 'beloved'. Other forms: Aimee, Amie.

Anastasia: (Greek) 'resurrection'.
Pet form: Stacey.

Andrea: (Greek) 'manly'. The feminine version of **Andrew**, from the Italian form *Andrea*. Other forms: Andra, Andria, Andrina, Dreena, Rea, Rena.

Angela: (Greek) 'messenger'.
Other forms: Angelena, Angeline.

Anita, Nita: See **Ann**.

Ann(e), Anna, Annie, Hannah: (Hebrew)
'grace'. **Hannah** is the original form. The
French form **Anne** is now more commonly
used. Other forms: Anita, Annetta, Annette,
Nan, Nanette, Neta, Nina, Nita.

Annabel: (Latin) 'lovable'. Or possibly a
compound of **Anna** and the Latin word *bella*,
meaning 'beautiful'. Pet forms: Bel, Bella,
Belle.

Annette, Annetta: See **Ann**.

Annice, Annis: See **Agnes**.

Antonia: (Latin) feminine
form of **Antony**, derived
from the Roman clan
name *Antonius*. Other
forms: Antoinette (French),
Antonette, Antonica, Tanya,
Tonia, Tonya.

April: (Latin) from the name of the month.
Other form: Avril (French).

Arabella: Possibly (Latin) 'beautiful altar'.
Pet forms: Bel, Bell, Bella, Belle.

Audrey: Shortened form of the
Old English name *Ethelreda*,
meaning 'noble' and 'strength'.

Aurora, Aurore: (Latin) 'dawn'.
Other form: Dawn.

Avril: See **April**.

B

Babette: See **Elizabeth**.

Barbara, Barbra: (Latin) 'foreign, stranger'.
Pet forms: Bab, Babs, Barbie, Barby, Bobbie.

Beatrice, Beatrix: (Latin) 'bringer of
happiness'. Pet forms: Bee, Beatty, Trix, Trixie.

Belinda: (Old German) 'serpent-like'.
Pet forms: Bel, Linda, Lindy.

Bel, Bell, Belle, Bella: See **Annabel**,
Arabella, **Belinda** and **Isabella**.

Berenice: See **Bernice**.

Bernadette: (Old German) 'bear-hard'. The
feminine form of **Bernard**.

Bernice, Berenice: (Greek) 'bringer of victory'.

Bertha: (Old German) 'bright'.
Pet forms: Bert, Berta, Bertie.

Beryl: (Greek) from the gem name.

Bess, Bessie, Beth, Betsy, Bettina, Betty: See
Elizabeth.

Beverly, Beverley: (Old English) 'of the
beaver-meadow'.

Bonnie, Bonny: (Latin) 'good'.

Brenda: (Old Norse) 'a sword'.

Bridget: (Celtic) 'strength'. The
name of a Celtic fire goddess,
an Irish saint. Pet form: Biddy.

Bronwen: (Welsh)
'white breast'.

Camilla: (Latin) 'attendant at a sacrifice'. Pet forms: Cammie, Millie, Milly.

Candida: (Latin) 'white'. Other forms: Candice, Candy.

Carla: (Old German) 'free woman'. Feminine version of *Carl*, which is a German form of **Charles**. Other forms: Carlene, Carley, Carlie.

Carmel: (Hebrew) 'the garden'. The name of a mountain in the Holy Land associated in the Bible with the Virgin Mary.

Carmen: (Latin) 'song'. Also the Spanish form of **Carmel**. Other forms: Carmine.

Carol, Carola, Caroline, Carolyn: (Old German) 'free woman'. The feminine version of *Carlo*, which is the Italian form of **Charles**. Other forms: Caddy, Carey, Carrie, Lyn, Lynne.

Cassandra: (Greek) 'confuser of men'. In Greek mythology, **Cassandra** was given powers of prophecy by the god Apollo. But she betrayed him so he put a curse on her, which caused her prophecies to be disbelieved. Pet forms: Cass, Cassy.

Catherine: (Greek) 'pure'. Other forms: Catalina (Spanish), Caterina (Italian), Catharine, Catherina, Cathleen, Catriona (Gaelic), Karen (Danish), Karin (Swedish), Katerina, Katharina (German), Kathleen, Kathryn, Katrina. Pet forms: Casey, Cathie, Cathy, Kate, Katie, Katy, Kathie, Kathy, Kay, Kit, Kittie, Kitty.

Catriona: See **Catherine**.

Cecilia, Celia: (Latin) 'blind'. Other forms: Cecily, Cicely, Se(e)lia, Sheelagh, Sheila, Sile, Sisley.

Celeste, Celestine: (Latin) 'heavenly'.

Chantal: Originally a French place-name, meaning 'stony place', used in honour of Saint Jeanne of *Chantal* (1572-1641). Other forms: Chantall, Chantel, Chantelle, Shantel, Shantell, Shantelle.

Charity: (Latin) 'Christian love'. One of the 'virtue' names.

Charlotte: (Old German) 'free woman'. The French feminine form of **Charles**. Other forms: Charleen, Charlotta. Pet forms: Charlie, Lottie, Lotty, Totty.

Charmaine: From the Roman clan name *Carmineus*. Other forms: Sharmaine, Sharmane.

Cherry: Derived from the name **Charity**.

Cheryl: Developed from the name **Cherry** in the 1920s, when **Beryl** was a popular name. Closely linked with the French words *chérie*, meaning 'dear' and *cerise*, meaning 'cherry'. Other forms: Cherilyn, Sheral, Sherry.

Chloe: (Greek) 'a green shoot'. In Greek mythology, a name given to the goddess Demeter, who protected the green fields. Other forms: Clea, Cloe.

Christiana: (Latin) 'follower of Christ'. The feminine form of **Christian**. Other forms: Christina, Christine, Kirsten, Kristin, Kristina. Pet forms: Chris, Chrissy, Kirsty, Kris, Krista, Krissy.

Christine: See **Christiana**.

Chrystal, Crystal: One of the jewel names.

Cindy, Cyndy: See **Cynthia**.

Clair(e), Clare: (Latin) 'clear' or 'famous'. One of the most popular girls' names. Other forms: Clara, Claribel, Clarinda, Clarrie.

Claudia: (Latin) 'lame'. The feminine form of **Claud**. Other forms: Claude, Claudine, Gladys (Welsh).

Clea: See **Chloe**.

Cleo: (Greek) 'glory' or 'father's fame'.

Cloe: See **Chloe**.

Coleen, Colleen: (Irish) 'girl'.

Colette: See **Nicola**.

Constance: (Latin) 'constant' or 'faithful'. Used in various forms throughout the ages — *Custance* in the Middle Ages, *Constancy* in the 17th century and *Constantia* in Victorian times. Pet forms: Con, Connie.

Cordelia: (Latin) 'warm-hearted'. Pet form: **Delia**.

Corin(ne): Probably from the Greek word *kore*, meaning 'a maiden'. Other forms: Corinna, Corrin.

Crystal: See **Chrystal**.

Cybil: See **Sibyl**.

Cynthia: (Greek) in Greek mythology, Artemis, the goddess of wild animals, hunting and forests, was sometimes called **Cynthia**. Other forms: Cindy, Cynthiana, Sindy.

D

Dagmar: (Danish) 'Dane's joy'.

Daisy: (Old English) 'day's eye'. From the name of the yellow-centred flowers, which open their petals by day and close them at night. Other form: Marguerite (French).

Dana: See **Daniella**.

Daniella: (Hebrew) 'God has judged'. The feminine form of **Daniel**. Other forms: Dana (Scandinavian), Danielle (French).

Daphne: (Greek) 'laurel bush' or 'bay tree'.

Dawn: See **Aurora**.

Deanna: See **Diana**.

Deborah: (Hebrew) 'bee' — symbolising wisdom and eloquence. Other forms: Debbra, Debora. Pet forms: Deb, Debbie.

Deirdre: (Irish) of uncertain meaning. Possibly 'one who rages' or 'broken-hearted'. In Irish mythology, the beautiful **Deirdre** eloped to Scotland only to commit suicide after her lover was murdered by the king.

Delia: (Greek) derived from the Greek island *Delos*, the legendary birthplace of the Greek goddess Artemis. See also **Cordelia**.

Denice, Denise: (Greek) feminine form of **Denis**, which is derived from *Dionysus*, the Greek god of wine.

Diana: (Latin) name of the Roman goddess equivalent to the Greek *Artemis*, goddess of animals, hunting and forests. Other forms: Deanna, Diane (French), Dianne.

Diane, Dianne: See **Diana**.

Dilys: (Welsh) 'perfect, genuine'.

Dolores: (Spanish) 'grief'. A short form of *Maria de los Dolores* 'Mary of the sorrows', one of the names given to the Virgin Mary. Pet forms: Lola, Lolita.

Dominica: (Latin) 'born on the Sabbath day'. The feminine form of **Dominic**.

Donna: (Italian) 'lady'. Sometimes used in conjunction with other names, for example *Donna-Maria*.

Dora: Originally a short form of **Dorothy**, now used independently.

Doreen, Dorene: Origin uncertain. Possibly (Irish) 'sullen' or from *Doireen*, the Irish form of **Dorothy**.

Doris: (Greek) of uncertain meaning. The name of a sea nymph in Greek mythology.

Dorothy: (Greek) 'gift of God'. Abbreviated to Dolly in the 16th century, the name was so popular that it became the name of a children's toy – *dolly*. Other forms: Doireen (Irish), Dorothea. Pet forms: Dodie, Dodo, Doll, Dolly, Dora, Dot, Dottie.

Dulcie: (Latin) 'sweet'.

Edith: (Old English) derived from the name *Eadgyth*, meaning 'prosperous' and 'war'. Pet forms: Eda, Ede, Edie, Edy.

Edna: Origin uncertain. Possibly derived from the Old English name *Edana*, meaning 'happy protection'.

Edwina: (Old English) 'rich friend'. The feminine form of **Edwin**.

Eileen, Eilean: See **Helen**.

Elaine: See **Helen**.

Eleanor: See **Helen**. Other forms: Eleanora, Eleanore, Elinor, Lenora, Lenore, Leonora, Leonore. Pet forms: **Ella**, **Nell**, Nellie, **Nora**, Norah.

Elizabeth, Elisabeth, Eliza: (Hebrew) 'oath of God'. One of the most popular girls' names, found in various forms throughout the world. Other forms: Elisa, Elisabetta (Italian), Elise (French and German), Elspeth, Ishbel (Scottish), Isabel (Spanish). Pet forms: Babette (French), Bess, Bessie, Bessy, Bet, Beth, Betsy, Bettina, Betty, Elsa, Ilse (German), Elsie (Scottish), Libby, Lis, Lisa, Lisbeth, Liz, Liza, Lizbeth, Lizzie.

Ella: (Old German) 'all, entirely'. Also a pet form of **Eleanor** and **Isabella** or other names ending in '-ella'.

Ellen: See **Helen**.

Elma: See **Wilhelmina**.

Elsa, Elsie, Elspeth: See **Elizabeth**.

Emily: (Latin) from the Roman clan name *Aemilius*. Other forms: Emilia, Emilie. Pet forms: Em, Emmy, Millie, Milly.

Emma: (Old German) 'universal'. The English form *Em* or *Emm* was more common until the mid 18th century.

Enid: (Welsh) possibly 'wood-lark'.

Erica, Erika: (Old Norse) 'sole ruler'. The feminine form of **Eric**.

Erin: (Irish) 'Ireland'. Other form: Erina.

Esther, Hester: (Persian) 'evening star'. Pet forms: Essie, Hetty.

Eunice: (Greek) 'happy victory'.

Eva, Eve: (Hebrew) 'life'. Pet form: Evie.

Evelyn, Evelina, Eveline: Origin uncertain. Possibly (Irish) 'pleasant'.

Faith: One of the 'virtue' names. Pet form: Fay.

Fay(e): (French) 'fairy' or 'faith'.

Felicity: (Latin) 'happiness'. Other forms: Felice, Felicia. Pet forms: Fee, Flic, Flick, Fliss.

Fenella: (Gaelic) 'white shoulder'. Other form: Finola. Pet forms: Fen, Fenny, Fin, Finny, Nuala (Irish).

Finola: See **Fenella**.

Fiona: (Gaelic) 'fair'. The original form was *Fionn*.

Fleur: (French) 'flower'.

Flora: (Latin) 'flower'. Name of the Roman goddess of flowers and the Spring. Pet forms: Flo, Florrie.

Florence: (Latin) 'blooming'. Pet forms: Flo, Florrie, Floss.

Frances: (Latin) 'Frenchwoman'. The feminine form of **Francis**. Other forms: Francesca (Italian), Francine (French), Francisca (Spanish). Pet forms: Fanny, Fran, Frankie, Frannie.

Frederica: (Old German) 'peaceful ruler'. The feminine form of **Frederick**. Pet forms: Fred, Freda, Frede, Rica.

Frieda: (Old German) 'peace'.

G

Gabrielle, Gabriella: (Hebrew) 'strong woman of God'. The feminine form of *Gabriel*. Pet forms: Gabe, Gabie, Gaby.

Gail: Originally a pet form of **Abigail**, now regarded as a name in its own right.

Gay(e): (English) 'happy, lively'.

Gaynor, Gaenor: (Welsh) of uncertain meaning. Derived from *Guinevere*, and now an independent name. See also **Jennifer**.

Gemma, Jemma: (Italian) 'a gem'.

Georgina: (Greek) 'farmer'. The feminine form of **George**. Other forms: Georgia, Georgiana, Georgette, Georgine. Pet form: George, Georgie, Gina.

Geraldine, Geraldene: (Old German) 'spear ruler'. The feminine form of **Gerald**. Pet forms: Gerrie, Gerry, Jerry.

Germaine: (French) 'German'.

Gillian, Jillian: (English) derived from the Latin name **Julian**, which means 'belonging to Julius'. It was so common in the Middle Ages that it was used generally to mean 'a girl'. Pet forms: Gill, Gilly, Jill, Jilly. See also **Juliana**.

Gladys: Anglicised form of *Gwladys*, the Welsh equivalent of **Claudia**. Pet form: Glad.

Glenda: (American) originated in the United States at the end of the 19th century. May have derived from **Glen** or **Gwen**.

Glennis, Glenys: See **Glynis**.

Gloria: (Latin) 'glory' or 'fame'.

Glynis: (Welsh) 'little valley'. Other forms: Glennis, Glenys.

Grace: (Latin) 'grace', 'thanks'. Until the 19th century *Gracia* was the preferred form.

Greta: See **Margaret**.

Gwen, Gwenda: (Welsh) 'white'.

Gwendalen: (Welsh) 'white circle'. Other forms: Gwendolen, Gwendoline, Gwendolyn. Pet forms: Gwen, Gwenda, Gwennie.

Gwyneth: (Welsh) 'blessed' or 'happy'. Pet forms: Gwinny, Gwyn.

Hannah: See **Ann**.

Harriet, Harriot: (Old German) originally the pet form of **Henrietta**. Now considered a separate name. Pet forms: Hattie, Hatty.

Hayley: English place-name and surname, meaning 'hay-meadow'.

Hazel: A plant name used as first name since the 19th century.

Heather: From the plant name.

Heidi: See **Adelaide**.

Helen: (Greek) 'the bright shining one'. Other forms: Aileen, Eilean, Eileen (Irish), Elaine, Eleanor (Old French), Ellen (Old English), Elena (Italian and Spanish), Helena (Latin), Hélène (French), Helene (German), Ilona (Hungarian). Pet forms: Hele, **Nell**, Nellie, Nelly.

Helga: (Norse) 'holy'. Other form: Olga (Russian).

Henrietta: (Old German) 'home ruler'. The feminine form of **Henry**. Pet forms: Etta, Etty, Henny, Hettie, Hetty.

Hester: See **Esther**.

Hilda, Hylda: (Old English) 'battle'.

Holly: From the plant name. Other forms: Holli, Hollie, Holley.

I

Ilona: See **Helen**.

Ilse: See **Elizabeth**.

Imogen: First appears in Shakespeare's play *Cymbeline*, thought to be a misprint of the name *Innogen* (Latin) meaning 'innocent'.

Ingrid: (Old Norse) 'Ing's ride'. *Ing* was the Norse god of fertility and crops, and his steed was a golden boar.

Inez, Ines: See **Agnes**.

Iona: From the name of the island in the Scottish Hebrides.

Irene: (Greek) 'peace'.

Iris: Goddess of the rainbow in Greek mythology. Also a plant name.

Isabel, Isabella, Isobel: See **Elizabeth**. Pet forms: Bel, Bell, Bella, Belle.

Ishbel: See **Elizabeth**.

Isla: A Scottish river name used as a first name.

Ivy: A plant name used as a first name since the 1860s.

J

Jacqueline, Jacquelyn: (Hebrew) 'supplanter' or 'deceiver'. Feminine form of *Jacques*, which is the French form of **Jacob**. Pet forms: Jackie, Jacky, Jacqui.

Jaime: (Hebrew) 'supplanter'. Spanish and Portuguese form of **James**, used as a girl's name since the 1970s. Other form: Jamie (Scottish).

Jan: See **Janet** and **Janice**.

Jane, Jean, Joan, Jo(h)anna, Joanne: (Hebrew) 'God is gracious'. Feminine forms of **John**. Other forms: Jeanne, Jeannette (French), Giovanna (Italian), Juana, Juanita (Spanish), Johanna (German), Seonad, Shona, Sine, Sheena (Gaelic), Sian (Welsh), Sinead (Irish). **Janet, Janice, Janie, Jean(n)ette** — now regarded as independent names. Pet forms: Jan, Janey, Janie.

Janet: See **Jane**. Earlier form *Janeta*. Other forms: Jenet, Janette, Jenetta, Jenette. Pet forms: Jan, Jess, Jessie, Jinty.

Janice, Janis: See **Jane**. First used in the 1890s. Pet form: Jan.

Janie, Janey: See **Jane**.

Jasmine: (Persian) from the flower name.

Jean: See **Jane**. Other forms: Jeanetta, Jeanette, Jeanie, Jeanine, Jeannette, Jeannie. Pet forms: Netta, Netti(e).

Jemima: (Hebrew) 'dove'. Pet forms: Jem, Jemmy, Mima.

Jemma: See **Gemma**.

Jennifer: (Welsh) 'fair, white' and 'yielding, smooth'. Derived from the name *Guinevere*. Other forms: Gaenor, Gaynor. Pet forms: Jen, Jenney, Jennie, Jenny.

Jerry: See **Geraldine**.

Jessica: (Hebrew) 'He beholds'. Pet forms: Jess, Jessie.

Jessie: See **Janet** and **Jessica**.

Jill: See **Gillian**.

Joan, Joanna, Joanne: See **Jane**. Other form: Siobhan (Irish).

Jocelyn, Joceline: Origin uncertain. Possibly (Latin) 'gay, sportive' or from *Joss*, a form of *Jodoc* (French), the name of an early Breton saint. Other form: Joyce.

Josephine: (Hebrew) 'God shall add'. From *Josepha*, the feminine form of **Joseph**. Pet forms: Jo, Joe, Josie, Jozy.

Joy: (Latin) 'joy'.

Joyce: See **Jocelyn**.

Judith: (Hebrew) 'a Jewess'. Pet forms: Jude, Judie, Judy.

Julia: (Latin) 'soft-haired'. The feminine form of *Julius*. Other form: Juliet. Pet forms: Judy (Irish), Julie (French).

Juliana, Julianna: (Latin) 'belonging to *Julius*'. The feminine forms of **Julian**. Other forms: Gillian, Jillian, Lianne. Pet forms: Gill, Gilly, Jill, Jilly, Julie, July.

Juliet: See **Julia**.

June: From the name of the month. Used as a first name since the beginning of the 20th century.

Justina, Justine: (Latin) 'righteous, just'. The feminine forms of **Justin**.

Karen, Karin: See **Catherine**: Other forms: Karena, Karina.

Katherine, Katheryn, Kathleen, Katie, Katrine, Kay(e): See **Catherine**.

Kelly: Origin uncertain. Possibly (Irish) 'strife', or a place-name in Devon, meaning 'wood', or from a Manx surname of Gaelic origin.

Kendra: Origin uncertain. Possibly a combination of **Kenneth** and **Alexandra** or **Sandra**.

Kerry: Irish place-name used as a first name.

Kim: (Old English) 'royally bold'. Also a boy's name.

Kimberley: From the town in South Africa, named after *Lord Kimberley*, whose surname derived from an English place-name meaning 'land belonging to Cyneburg'.

Kirsten, Kirsty, Krista: See **Christiana**.

Kylie: (Aboriginal) 'curled stick' or 'boomerang'. One of the most popular girls' names in Australia.

L

Laura: (Latin) 'laurel'. Other forms: Lauren, Lauretta, Laurinda, Lolly, Lora, Loretta.

Laverne: Probably after the Californian place-name *La Verne*.

Lavinia: Origin unknown. The name of the second wife of Aeneas, the son of the Roman goddess Aphrodite.

Layla: See **Leila**.

Leila, Layla: (Persian) 'dark-haired'.

Lenora, Lenore: See **Eleanor**.

Leonie: (Latin) 'lion'. The French feminine form of *Leon*, which is a form of **Leo**.

Lesley: Derived from the Scottish place-name and surname. Generally the feminine form of **Leslie**, although the male form is used for both boys and girls in the United States.

Letitia: (Latin) 'gladness'. The medieval form was *Lettice*. Other form: Luttuce. Pet forms: Lettie, Letty.

Lianne: See **Juliane**.

Libby: See **Elizabeth**.

Lilian: From the Italian word for the plant 'lily'. Other form: Lillian (American).

Lily: From the flower name or possibly derived from **Elizabeth**. Other forms: Lilie, Lilley, Lilly.

Linda: Originally appeared as an ending to many Germanic names, where '-linde' or '-linda' meant 'serpent', symbolising wisdom. Now a name in its own right. Pet forms: Lindy, Lyn, Lynn, Lynne.

Lindsey, Lynsey: A Scottish place-name and family name of the Earls of Crawford. **Lindsay** is the male form.

Lisa, Liza, Lisbeth, Liz, Lizzy: See **Elizabeth**.

Lois: Origin uncertain. Possibly (Greek) 'good'.

Lola, Lolita: See **Dolores**.

Loretta: See **Laura**.

Lorna: From the Scottish place-name *Lorn*.

Lorraine: (French) derived from the region of France.

Lottie: See **Charlotte**.

Louise, Louisa: (French) 'famous'. Feminine form of **Louis**.

Lucia: (Latin) from the Roman clan name *Lucius*, meaning 'light'. Other forms: Luce, Lucy, Lucinda, Lucilla, Lucil(l)e.

Lucile, Lucilla, Lucinda: See **Lucia**.

Lucky: Sometimes used for a girl born on Friday 13th.

Lucy: See **Lucia**.

Lydia: (Greek) 'woman of Lydia' – a region of Asia.

Lyn: Pet form of **Linda**, used independently since the 1940s. Other forms: Lynn, Lynne.

Mabel: Possibly from the French *ma belle*, 'my beautiful one'. Other forms: Mabelle, Mable, Maybel, Maybell, Maybelle.

Madeleine: See **Magdalene**. Pet forms: Mad, Maddie, Maddy.

Mae: See **May**.

Magdalene: (Hebrew) 'woman of Magdala', after *St Mary Magdalene*, who came from Magdala. Other forms: Madeleine (French), Malena (Danish).

Maisie: Scottish form of **Margery**, influenced by the Gaelic form *Marsail*. See **Margaret**.

Manda, Mandy: See **Amanda** and **Miranda**.

Marcella, Marcia: (Latin) feminine forms of **Marcus**. Derived from the Roman god of war, *Mars*.

Margaret: (Greek) 'pearl'. Other forms: Margarete (German), Margarita (Spanish), Margherita (Italian), Marguerite (French). Pet forms: Greta, Gretchen (German), Madge, Maggie, Maggy, Mags, Maisie (Scottish), Marge, Margery, Margot, Marjory, May, Meg, Meg(h)an (Welsh), Meggy, Meta, Mysie, Peg, Peggie, Peggy, Rita.

Margery: See **Margaret**. Pet form: Marge.

Maria, Marie: See **Mary**.

Marian, Marion, Marianne: See **Mary**. Other forms: Mary-Ann, Maynie, Mysie.

Marilyn: A combination of **Mary** and **Ellen**.

Marsha: (American) phonetic form of **Marcia**.

Martha, Marta: (Aramaic) 'lady, mistress of the house'. Pet forms: Marti, Martita, Matty.

Martina: (Latin) 'belonging to Mars'. The feminine form of **Martin**. Pet form: Marty.

Mary: Anglicised form of the Hebrew name **Miriam**, meaning 'wished for child' or 'rebellion'. Other forms: Maria (Spanish), Marie, Marian(ne), Marion(ne) (French), Mari (Gaelic), Maire (Irish), Moira, Moyra (Welsh), Marilyn, Maureen. Pet forms: Mally, Minnie, Moll, Molly, Poll, Polly.

Mat(h)ilda: (Old German) 'battle-mighty'.
Pet forms: Mat, Matty, Maud(e), Patty, Tilly,
Tilda.

Maureen: See **Mary**.

Mavis: (Old English) 'song thrush'.

Maxime: (French) from the Latin word
maxima, meaning 'the greatest'.

Maxine: Modern feminine form of **Max**.

May, Mae: Pet form of **Mary** and **Margaret**.
Also connected with the name of the month.

Meg(h)an: See **Margaret**.

Melanie: (Greek) 'black, dark complexioned'.
Earlier form *Melania*.

Melicent: See **Millicent**.

Melinda: (Latin) 'honey', with the fashionable
18th century ending '-inda'.

Melissa: (Greek) 'bee'.

Meryl: Phonetic form of **Muriel**. Other forms:
Merrilee, Merill, Merrily.

Mia: (Italian/Spanish) 'my'.

Michelle, Michele: (Greek) 'Who is like the
Lord?' From the French form of **Michael**.

Millicent, Melicent: (Old German) 'noble
strength'. Pet forms: Millie, Milly.

Millie, Milly: Pet forms of **Amelia**, **Camilla**,
Emily and **Millicent**.

Mirabel: (Latin) 'wonderful'.

Miranda: (Latin) 'fit to be admired'.
Pet forms: Manda, Mandy.

Miriam: See **Mary**.

Moira, Moyra: See **Mary**.

Molly: See **Mary**.

Mona: (Irish) 'noble'.

Monica: Origin uncertain.
Possibly (Greek) 'alone' or
(African) the name of St Augustine's mother.

Morag: (Gaelic) 'great'.

Muriel: (Irish) 'sea-bright'.

Myfanwy: (Welsh) 'my fine one'.

Myra: Invented by the 17th century poet Fulke
Greville (1554-1628). Possibly from the Latin,
meaning 'sweet-smelling oil', or as an anagram
of **Mary**.

Nadia: (Russian) 'hope'. Other form: Nadine
(French).

Nan, Nance, Nancy, Nanette: See **Agnes** and
Ann.

Naomi: (Hebrew) 'pleasant', 'delight'.

Natalie: (Latin) 'birthday of the Lord'. First
appeared in the 1880s. *Natalia* was the original
form. Other form: Natasha (Russian). Pet
forms: Nat, Nattie, Natty.

Nell: Pet form of **Helen** and **Eleanor**, used independently since the 17th century. Other forms: Nella, Nellie, Nelly.

Nessa, Nessie, Nesta: See **Agnes**.

Netta: Pet form of **Annetta** and other names ending in '-etta' and '-ette'. Also used independently.

Nicola: (Greek) 'victory of the people'. From the Italian form of **Nicholas**, used as a girl's name in Britain since the 1940s. Other form: Nicole (French). Pet forms: Colette (French), Nicki, Nicky.

Nina, Nita: See **Ann**.

Noelle, Noeleen: (French) 'Christ's birthday'. The feminine form of **Noel**, used since the 1950s.

Nora, Norah: Pet form of **Eleanor**, also used independently. Other forms: Noreen (Irish), Noreena, Norene.

Norma: (Latin) 'pattern' or 'model'.

Nuala: See **Fenella**.

Octavia: (Latin) 'eight'. Pet forms: Tave, Tavy.

Olga: See **Helga**.

Olive: (Latin) 'olive' – the symbol of peace. Other form: Olivia.

Olwen: (Welsh) 'white footprint'. In Welsh legend, wherever the beautiful maiden **Olwen** trod, four white clover leaves sprang from the ground.

Oona, Oonagh: See **Una**.

Ophelia: (Greek) 'help, aid'. Possibly influenced by the Roman clan name *Ofellius*.

Oriana: (Latin) 'dawn, sunrise'.

Paige: From the surname, now used as a first name.

Pamela: Origin uncertain. Possibly (Greek) 'all honey'. Or possibly a literary invention of Sir Philip Sidney (1554-1586). Pet form: Pam.

Patricia: (Latin) 'noble'. The feminine form of **Patrick**. Other form: Patrice (French). Pet forms: Pat, Patsy, Patti, Patty, Tricia, Trisha.

Paula: (Latin) 'small'. The feminine form of **Paul**. Other forms: Paulette, Pauline (French).

Pauline: See **Paula**.

Penelope: (Greek) 'bobbin' or 'weaver'. Pet forms: Pen, Penny.

Perdita: (Latin) 'lost'.

Peta, Pete, Petra: (Greek) 'stone, rock'. The feminine forms of **Peter**.

Petula: (Latin) 'sauciness'. Pet form: Pet.

Philadelphia: (Greek) 'brotherly love'. Pet forms: Del, Fee, Phil.

Philippa: (Greek) 'fond of horses'. The feminine form of **Philip**. Pet forms: Philly, Pip, Pippa.

Philomena: (Greek) 'I am loved' or 'strong in friendship'. Pet form: Phil.

Phoebe: (Greek) 'pure, bright'. The name of the Greek goddess of the moon. Other forms: Pheabe, Phebe.

Phyllis: (Greek) 'foliage'. In Greek mythology **Phyllis** changed into an almond tree when she died. Other forms: Phillida, Phillis, Phyllida. Pet forms: Phil, Phyl.

Polly: Originally a pet name for **Mary**, used independently since the 18th century.

Pollyanna: Compound name from **Polly** and **Anna**.

Poppy: Flower name, used as a first name since the late 19th century.

Priscilla: (Latin) 'old, primitive'. Other forms: Precilla, Pricilla. Pet form: Cilla.

Prudence: One of the 'virtue' names. Pet forms: Pru, Prue.

Queen, Queenie, Queeny: The title used as a first name.

Rachel: (Hebrew) 'ewe' – symbolising innocence. Other forms: Rachelle (French), Raquel (Spanish and Portuguese). Pet forms: Rae, Raelene, Raye.

Raina, Raine: (German) 'mighty army'. The feminine form of **Rayner**.

Raquel: See **Rachel**.

Rebecca(h): (Hebrew) of uncertain meaning. Possibly 'knotted card'. One of the most popular girls' names. Pet forms: Becca, Beckie, Becky.

Rhian: (Welsh) 'maiden'.

Rhoda: (Greek) 'rose'. Originally given to girls born on Rhodes – the Greek island of 'roses'.

Rhona, Rona: (Old Norse) possibly from the Scottish place-name, meaning 'rough island'.

Rhonwen: (Welsh) 'pike' or 'lance' and 'fair'. Probably implying slender.

Rita: Pet form of **Margaret** and names ending in '-rita'. Used independently since the early 20th century.

Roberta: (Old German) 'fame, bright'. Feminine form of **Robert**, first used in the 1870s. Other forms: Robina, Robinn, Robyn. Pet forms: Bobbie, Bobby.

Roisin, Rosheen: (Irish) 'rose'.

Romy: See **Rosemary**.

Rosa: (Latin) 'rose'. Other form: Rosalie (French).

Rosalind, Rosaline: (Old German) 'horse serpent' or (Spanish) 'pretty rose'. Pet forms: Rosie, Rosy.

Rosamond, Rosamund: (Old German) 'horse protection' or (Latin) 'pure rose'. Pet forms: Rosie, Rosy.

Rosanna, Roseanne: Compound name from **Rose** and **Anne**.

Rose: (Old German) 'fame'. Now more commonly associated with the flower name.

Rosemary: Possibly a combination of **Rose** and **Mary** or from the name of the herb, which means 'herb of the sea'. Other form: Rosemarie (French). Pet forms: Romy, Rosie, Rosy.

Rowena: (Celtic) 'white skirt'.

Roxana: (Latin) from the Persian name meaning 'the dawn'. Other forms: Roxane, Roxanne.

Ruby: The jewel name used as a first name. Other forms: Rubey, Rubie, Rubina.

Ruth: (Hebrew) possibly 'vision of beauty' or 'truth'.

Sabina, Sabine: (Latin) 'woman of the Sabine tribe'. Pet forms: Bina, Sabby.

Sabrina: (Latin) 'the boundary line'. The Roman name for the River *Severn* between England and Wales.

Sacha, Sasha: See **Alexandra**.

Sallianne: See **Sally-Ann**.

Sally: Originally a pet form of Sarah, used independently since the 18th century.

Sally-Ann: Compound name from **Sally** and **Ann(e)**. Other forms: Sallianne, Sallian.

Salome: (Hebrew) 'peace'.

Samantha: Origin is uncertain. Possibly from the Aramaic, meaning 'a listener'. Pet forms: Sam, Sammy.

Sandra, Sandy, Sandie: See **Alexandra**.

Sarah, Sara: (Hebrew) 'princess'. One of the most popular girls' names. Pet forms: Sadie, Sal, Sally.

Sasha, Sacha: See **Alexandra**.

Se(e)lia: See **Cecilia**.

Selina, Selinda: Origin uncertain. Possibly (Greek) after the goddess of the moon or (Latin) from the name *Coelina*, meaning 'heaven'.

Shan(a): (Hebrew) 'God is gracious'. The feminine form of **Shane** or a variant of **Sian**, the Welsh form of **Jane**. Other form: Shanita.

Shanita: See **Shan**.

Shantel, Shantell, Shantella: See **Chantal**.

Sharmaine, Sharmane: See **Charmaine**.

Sharon: (Hebrew) 'the plain'. Other forms: Sharan, Sharen, Sharin, Sharron. Pet form: Shari.

Sheena: See **Jane**. Other forms: Sheenagh, Sheona, Shiana.

Sheila, Sheelagh: See **Cecilia**.

Shelly: English place-name and surname, meaning 'meadow on a slope or ledge'. Used as a first name for boys and girls.

Sheral: See **Cheryl**.

Sheree, Shereen, Sheri: Anglicised form of the French word *chérie*, meaning 'dear'.

Shirley: English place-name, meaning 'bright clearing'. Originally a boy's name, used as a girl's name since the 1860s.

Shona, Shonagh: See **Jane**.

Sian: See **Jane**.

Sibyl, Sybil, Sybille: From the Greek mythological priestess. Other form: Cybil. Pet form: Sib.

Sile: See **Cecilia**.

Silvia, Sylvia: (Latin) 'wood'.

Simone: (Greek) 'snub-nosed'. The feminine form of **Simon**.

Sindy: See **Cynthia**. Other forms: Cindy, Cyndy.

Sinead: See **Jane**.

Siobhan: See **Joan**. Other forms: Chavon, Chavoni, Chevon, Chivon, Shavon, Shevon, Shivohn.

Sonia: See **Sophia**.

Sophia, Sophie: (Greek) 'wisdom'. Other forms: Sonia, Sonya (Russian), Sonja (Scandinavian).

Stacey: See **Anastasia**.

Stella: (Latin) 'star'.

Stephanie: (Greek) 'crown'. The feminine form of **Stephan**, introduced to Britain in the 1920s. *Stephania* was the original form. Pet forms: Steph, Stephy.

Sukey: See **Susan**.

Susan, Susanna(h): (Hebrew) 'lily'. Other forms: Susanne (German), Suzanna, Suzanne (French). Pet forms: Sue, Suke, Sukey, Susie, Susy.

Tabitha, Tabatha: (Aramaic) 'gazelle'.

Tamsin: See **Thomasin**. Pet forms: Tam, Tammie.

Tanya, Tania: See **Antonia** and **Tatiana**.

Tara: (Irish) 'hill'.

Tatiana, Tatania: (Russian) from *Tatius*, a king of the Sabines. Other forms: Tania, Tanya, Tonia, Tonya.

Tegwen: (Welsh) 'beautiful' and 'fair'.

Teresa, Theresa: Origin disputed. Possibly connected with the Greek island of *Therasia* or the Greek word meaning 'harvest'. Other forms: Terese, Thérèse (French), Theresia (German). Pet forms: Tess, Tessa, Tessy, Tracey, Tracy.

Tess, Tessa, Tessy: See **Teresa**.

Thelma: (Greek) 'will'.

Thomasin(a): (Hebrew) 'twin'. The feminine form of **Thomas**. The form **Tamsin** is now more popular. Pet form: Zena.

Thora, Thyra: (Old Norse) 'Thor battle'.

Tiffany: (Greek) 'manifestation of God'. Sometimes given to girls born on 6th January – Epiphany.

Tilly: See **Mat(h)ilda**.

Tina: Pet form of names ending '-tina', such as **Martina**. Used independently since the beginning of the 20th century.

Tonya: See **Antonia** and **Tatiana**.

Trac(e)y: See **Teresa**.

Tricia, Trisha: See **Patricia**.

Trudi, Trudie, Trudy: Pet form of names ending in '-trude'. Used independently since the 1940s.

Ula: (Old English) 'owl'.

Una: (Irish) 'lamb'. Anglicised as **Agnes** or **Unity**. Other forms: Oona, Oonagh.

Unity: The word used as a name. Other forms: Una, Unita, Unite.

Ursula: (Latin) 'little she-bear'.

Val: See **Valerie**.

Valda: Feminine form of the Slavic name *Valdemar*, common in Yugoslavia and Scandinavia.

Valentia: (Latin) 'strong, healthy'. Other forms: Valence, Valencia, Valentina, Valentine.

Valerie: (Latin) 'to be strong'. Pet form: Val.

Vanessa, Vanesse: Originally a literary invention by Jonathan Swift (1667-1745) from the name *Esther Van*homrigh.

Vashti: (Persian) 'beautiful'.

Vera: (Latin) 'true'.

Veronica: Origin uncertain. Possibly (Latin) 'true image' or from the Greek name **Berenice**. Also a flower name.

Victoria: (Latin) 'victory'. The feminine form of **Victor**. Pet forms: Vicki, Vickie, Vicky.

Violet: The flower name used as a first name.

Virginia: (Latin) feminine form of the Roman clan name *Verginius*, also associated with the Latin for 'maiden'. Pet forms: Ginger, Ginny, Jinny.

Vivien: (Latin) 'living, alive'. The feminine form of **Vivian**. Other forms: Vivianne, Vivienne.

Wanda: (Slavic) connected with the Germanic tribe, the *Vandals*.

Wendy: Literary invention of James Barrie in his book *Peter Pan* (1904), after a child suggested to him the phrase *'friendy-wendy'*. Other form: Wenda.

Wilhelmina, Williamina: (Old German) 'resolute protector'. The feminine forms of **William**. Pet forms: Elma, Mina, Minnie, Wilma.

Winifred: (Welsh) 'blessed reconciliation'. Pet forms: Win, Winnie.

Xenia: (Greek) 'hospitable'. Pronounced *zen-y-a*. Other forms: Zena, Zene, Zina.

Yolanda, Yolande: (Greek) 'violet'. Other form: Iolanthe (French).

Yvette, Yvonne: Origin is uncertain. Possibly (German) 'yew'. Other forms: Evon, Evonne.

Zandra: See **Alexandra**.

Zara: (Arabic) 'splendour', 'brightness of the East'. In European literature, the name is often given to Arabian princesses.

Zena, Zene, Zina: See **Xenia**.

Zoe: (Greek) 'life'.

Zola: (Italian) from the surname, meaning 'clod of the earth'.